CHILDREN OF APARTNESS

by Elaine Upton

Washington Writers' Publishing House
Washington, D.C.

Many people and spirits have helped bring this book to fulfillment. Special thanks to Maxine Clair for her careful, insightful, and loving reading of all of these poems; to Toi Derricote for her encouragement and enthusiasm; to Marc Widerschien for his faithful sharing over years; to Daisy Aldan, who has long believed in me; and to many members of the Washington Writers' Publishing House, who supported my work—particularly to Jean Nordhaus, to Ann Knox for production, and to Elaine Magarrell for publicity.

Publication of this book is possible thanks to grants from the Max and Victoria Dreyfus Foundation, the Jenny McKean Moore Fund for Writers, and The Prince Charitable Trusts, as well as donations from the many Friends of Washington Writers' Publishing House. It was funded in part by the D.C. Commission on the Arts and the National Endowment for the Arts.

Cover design by Jeanne Krohn
Typesetting by Barbara Shaw

Library of Congress Cataloging-in-Publication Data
Upton, Elaine Maria, 1945-
    Children of apartness / by Elaine Maria Upton.
        p.   cm.
    ISBN 0-931846-43-9
    I. Title.
PS3571.P455C47   1993
811'.54–dc20   93-7011
                                                  CIP

WASHINGTON WRITERS' PUBLISHING HOUSE   P.O. Box 15271   Washington, DC 20003

For Amy and Alvin Upton,
for the children—old and young—
who bring me home, and for
Lorraine with all her light.

Contents

Prologue

I THE WAY CHILDREN CALL

II BEYOND THE BORDERS

III DIASPORA

This
is about words.
Children are words.

Children are words
in the beginning
before truth
before falsehood
words from the womb
from the Primal Mother
from the Void.

This is about words.
Children
are words.

I
THE WAY CHILDREN CALL

Children Of Apartness

some hours i am afraid
perhaps i do not belong anymore. my brothers
gang boys in the streets of los angeles
mow hispanic boys down
or themselves never
grow up like summer grass
in drought. this need
for othering! this need
for death. we poets
have failed again.
where were we when
young mothers with five-inch fake
brass earrings fled
from hospital wards abandoning
half-born babies who soon
very soon grow old?
the B-52's perform
at merriweather post pavilion
all weekend. the Violent Femmes
are opening the show the paper says.
what can i say?
i drink bottled water. the label reads
from a mountain spring in maine.
far away places are also where
they make cocaine.

last week the police-
woman pushed away my path

with the back of her hand. she said
turn around go back it's not safe
here. who does she think
i am?
its just some
with ketchup fries and gun
or who do i think
she is? i am lost
amid words.

To June Jordan, From South Africa

In Brooklyn (was it?) you wrote:
I am waiting for the call.

Did you dream of a century of battles?
Or dream of incorrigible births?
Did you hear in another language,
mellifluous as hills?

Did you dream of low ceilings, closed
rooms, sweat, anger like the electricity
shut off for a season or a year?
Or of the feet of wayward boys
(and what is the way?), the feet
of men whom brightness
left like swift clouds, casting
a flat shadow in dust? Did you dream
of black and coloured police
implicit in their own oppression?
Did you dream of women who cut the cord
and heard the crying of babies already
too old for milk? Did you feel
the rhythms of desperate poems
hijacked from a sister's treachery?
Are you waiting still?

June, I call you
the way skin calls skin
the way wave calls wave
the way woman calls woman
the way children call
from before their births—forever.
I call.

i live

in the country
that side
when i'm not too tired
on sunday
i sometime see a chameleon
unwabu i call it
slowly movin cross the road
tip-toeing
quiet
and i wonder how long
it been doin that kinda thing
crossin the road
and i can never tell
if it look at me

otherwise
i be just sittin on the stoop
but i like the sun
so hot and near it hum
kinda like my ma
singin to me and i'm just all right
when i be alone.

        i live in the township.
        my new wheels with air and tape
        (and this girl   she like me)
        then the burning
        of somebody's house
        the yellow smoke real slow
        after all that heat and speed
        the flashing blade

of siren lights
day or dark don't matter
and my friend
he dead
these
are the main changes i know.

overcoming anthropology

in Natal
they say
there's a mountain
you can't point at
spirits are busy there
and in the Kalahari
the Bush people hear
the stars hunting
they say.
i saw naked breasts
of ripe unmarried girls
with long canes
as plentiful as acacia in their
hands
measuring the hills   already
for the ancestors' journeys
with the same canes
of acacia
it seemed to me
i saw myself and you
before i left
there
after
we bled for centuries
and returned

Heartbeats Under the Present Regime

Pretoria, 1989

We ride along
in a new machine
in the smooth streets
afraid of touching
the wrong button.

Zakele Ntuli

One of the last
traditional African drummers
they say.
Arms like spaghetti
but spaghetti can't fly.
A handshake like something
that other people do. He
cannot be reduced to
comparisons.
He prefers perhaps
the cigarette on his lips.

Feature Articles

Annual
I will change the names
to protect the guilty.
Or
I will not
change the names.

How much history
can a name bear: Vorster
Smuts DeKlerk?
Like how much reason
can a poem
bear?

This is a country
confusing refusing
or forgetting
or learning
how to speak

Learning
from the drought in December
detentions   "five year plans"
dramatic monologues
of advocates
who read
Shakespeare at Stellenbosch
I heard
the Nazi's did too.

Listen
some parts of the news change
every season.
Thank God in Africa the rain
doesn't lie.

Sundays.
I hear the rooster crow
the birds coo or chatter.
Then the instant colors
of the ice cream truck
tinkling through
the country roads.
This frightens the snakes
mutes the hiss.

Then children steal
ostrich eggs and laugh
—their voices thin
like mountain air. The women
walk along the roads
babies and dust
hugging their backs.

To me they sing
"dumela!"*
as though our God
will never leave.

* *Dumela* is a Northern Sotho word of greeting.

Weekdays.
On their knees
they scrub and sway
slowly singing
in Zulu or Sotho
now   and then
when *Baas* comes
they polish the tables
in Afrikaans.

It's almost natural
like swallowing
a chemist's pill
or a baby dying.

Notes Of An English Teacher

I play the kind executioner.
They look to me for salvation,
the common unknown poison,
verb, noun, exclamation.

"What is a sentence?" I ask.
"Words with complete thought,"
is the reply they mouth, and I
nod my head and sigh.

What wonder have I wrought!
What politic evasion of mission!

Oh, I pray to be purer and simpler!
And what *is* a sentence, I ask.

Maasai Warrior

The smooth surface of the photograph
covers the rough ground under your toes
—they do not bleed. They seem one with the ground.
You pose and I think to dissect your face.
Is it one more mask whose motions I do not understand?

The camera crowds an otherwise agile air
and the professor notes your warrior's arms
carrying a fan of *leleshwa* leaves
perfume we assume   forgetting?
Do your nostrils defy these notions of love?
Perhaps they welcome nothing we can name.

I can only imagine you
breathing low where the elephant falls
afraid not of the elephant but the spirit
of the elephant. I imagine your limbs
like a revelation of light   your heart neither hot
nor cold but blazing with the sun

and for all the bronze ballast of your bones
do you hide a woman in your side?
Perhaps your being a warrior (no other)
is somebody's salvation and the shield
before the camera one more mask.

Hand-Me-Downs

dresses in splattered bags
her mother brought home.
leftover cold duck
once. they preferred afterall

                     chicken wings.

nursery rhymes in tags
of yellow and red. a dream
of a room full of luck.
a room unseen afterall.

                     things

do not make rhymes. rags
are yellow and red. a dream
is no room full of luck
is no room at all.

Here In The Red Soil Of Africa

weeds grow in my little garden.
But I learn from
Kathrine Khumalo next door
to bend my hips, loosen my thighs, let
my sweat flow. My feet
almost hug and raise the ground
like when I kiss or dance.

And I have decided
that any lover
I might come to hold
will eat
from my bruised brown hands.
I will fill her thighs with rain
—flowers
and fruit of this land.

Children Of The Fontein Farm School

District Cullinan, South Africa

We were meant
to go beyond everything
pain   laughter
desire
the spread of wings   flight   height
our names.

A Rose By Any Other Name

Malehabe Thlopane
(in the non-racial school)
plays Juliet, a Capulet
—fourteen years old last night
a sword already in her breast.

And what was her name
when they spoke
it at home? The syllables
always changed at school.

At the school's Hall
ivy and calendula grow.
Ivy is obviously constant.
Calendula, however,
brings joy. She

speaks still
like a bright angel.
Like her I must
make a name for love.

Amfortas*

or something like a love and lament for Europe

I heard only your name
and that you were wounded.
I heard the sound of your name
—forward, open and strong.

I wondered if I would see you
and if you suffered still.
Was your story Mary Magdalen's,
or what if I said "Linda Brent"?

What if I said Nkrumah, Sobukwe
or the woman who married Sobukwe?
In Africa, the dead tell
the time. But you are the one I read

in school. So I took your wounds,
your name. Scattered syllables of my
self. And now I wake with the dead
and maybe still your strange love.

* In the Parceval legend, Amfortas is the wounded Fisher
King, of whom Parceval fails to ask the healing question.

oh be

at least human in the night
if in the day
you must wear a face
official as the noon sun

in the night
be on your knees
or weep for your mother
and let your eyes trace
the simple hunger in mine

A Lesson From My African (Male) Students

"The men and boys boil
and drink the blood
of the slaughtered cow,"
they tell me,
proudly.
"The women do not drink."

And my
woman (American)
mouth
is (to say the least)
relieved!

What Is A Poem? What Is Home?

After Lorraine Ndlovu's interviews with children

Christinah Somo—health: eyes good.
Headache sometimes. Once treated for TB.
She hears and understands but she forgets
things. Even when sent to the store for food.

No time to study. No time
to learn. Even in the heat
she aches with cold. Mother
father drink and fight. Sweat.

Sello Mashiane—he stays with relatives. Sometimes
he visits home but the parents are away to sell
the *baas's* eggs. He sleeps on the floor.
The dung is warm and the hair mites are gone.

Flaubert visited Paris
and hated humanity. Here
there's the story of the father
who steals the money saved
for the children's milk.

September summer is coming.
Does anyone hear the thunder
or does it travel past
like a shadow
without greeting?

"The South African Black Male Worker"
And *Baas's* Declaration

"The South African black male worker," *Baas* declares,
"cannot conceptualize a job from beginning to end."
But then, does he conceptualize the smooth tongues
of streets: Pretorius one-way in and Schoeman
out, Church (or Kerk) Street two-way
in and out, with jacarandas imported for spring?

Does he conceptualize milking the cows by machine,
selling the milk to Hatfield Dairies,
sanitizing the milk after Louis Pasteur,
eating his lunch of atchar in the reversed
elegance of a dark mine? Or making tiered
gardens and tiered tables for Parliament to decide

if he may live or die? Does he conceptualize
in English or Russian or Afrikaans?
Or in the plated terms of a police battalion?
Does he calculate the excrement of his empty stomach?
Does he see that a white man "discovered"
Africa? Does he know that he rises everyday

beaten, conquered and undiscovered?
Does he hear the decades of sentences pronounced
on his head? The dogs that bark when he walks
in the night? The damage of whisky and old
dirt? Does he conceptualize that he, like a thorny
cactus with a shy bloom in the night

might be one who remains
after we have tamed the rivers,
after we exhaust the rain.

I Am Branded

with sonnets, iambics, Shelley,
and love. The world is so white,
like the cliffs of Dover
in mists, like all
the bathers on Durban beaches.

South Africa/Azania

I have wanted
to love you, wanted
to have some place to love.
Of you, I have wanted
to ask, what is love?
What is loving you?
I have wanted the courage
to live with you, who seem
to say that living is dying.
This daily dying,
this giving my blood
to you,
is living.

I have wanted some Earth
where the gods could gather their words
like your hills making scrolls to oceans
at the edge
of the world. I have wanted
words like tamed and untamed
grasses playing on your veld.
I have wanted to listen.

I have wanted to know
what is wanting.
It is not your flags
I have wanted.
I call the colors of your day,
your skies blue with a bloody
sun and dark. I call
not to Europe's fair angels above,

but to clouds that gather
the icy light of pain.

I have wanted to know
boys in the streets of Sunnyside-
Pretoria, begging, stealing.
(I heard one
sigh
in nobody's tongue.)
And could I ever know
the weight of the bones
of thin laboring men
whose duty is to bend
and not to understand?

I have wanted to hear
the slim voices
of girls with blossoming breasts
and the throats of old women
—their faces falling
petal by burning petal
like roses yielding to winter.

I have wanted to feel the rhythms
of nests built between thorns
in a thorn tree,
the rhythms of weeding
in the black and red soils
for corn.

I have wanted to see our fear
of your ancient fertility,

of your naked love.
Azania,
I have wanted
what is wanting in me.

Let me see
your copper dust
and your long skies
at evening, red
with a thousand million wounds
and burning still!

Night Hike

Worlds wait in dark
emptying the hours for light.
Cows in the peace of a pasture
kneel and close in sleep.
From infant gold and cloud-laced
the spring moon turns silver
rises   cries out   is erased.

> From the deep an owl breathes,
> its melancholy marking time.

II
BEYOND THE BORDERS

In Brooklyn Heights
After Leaving South Africa

All that is left
is the artifice of night
and fear.
Your face and mine
and all of theirs,
the voiceless phantoms.
Oh speak! Or are you
in the silent bleeding moon
still striving West
beyond this decaying harbor
to some perfect order?

I will remember
how you came to me.
Do the drums still
rage and stop short
of madness, beat softly
in that different night?

Oceans

I look to oceans for words
or to seaweed in sand
that means nothing   but seaweed
and sand. the beach seems
a sheet   a gray
in winter an inhuman span. a scallop
shell that means only. not even food.
that once was water or light
or fingers perhaps that scarcely write.

The Last Of Summer Sun

fades from my hand
and rows of bonfires on the beach
fall to embers   then
the gray empty sand.

I think of you   the wistful wave
of late autumn   or sudden November
storm in my mind. But memory too
cools and the wind cries from afar.

Reading An Umberto Eco Novel

Some of us didn't die when the bullets were fired.
We survived but how? Running up a hill in a film
to the traitor's side? And now life is decaffeinated
coffee in a stained cup in the afternoon
—order in the hum of the refrigerator motor.
Otherwise, the bellicose terminology of the immune
system. Wars in our bodies. Deferred
for tax retirement plans. Our attention-span
is short says the Reverend King. From Castro to Japan
to the local bank and back again.
Whatever we say is second-hand. A Chinese female
sitting in for Dan Rather. Our plants in measured pots
in our living rooms. Routine pirouettes for children.
A little gin. Love between the tulips in the Sheraton Inn.
We have countless collector's items
in our minimum security prisons. It is only the dead
who are naked, the dead who travel so many places.
We forget—they still toss with demons
and imperceptibly turn with evolutionary angels.

Poems Do Not Come From Safe Places

Take January in Iraq, when the U.S. broke
over Baghdad's sky: how many babies,
taken from drips and incubators, died?
How many doctors' hands were stunned
when new mothers panicked and fled
while the sky shrieked and cried
in an unknown tongue? I tell you
the doctors' masks are in the streets
on soldiers' mouths. And smoke
is another screen in all our minds.

April In Northern Virginia

I have come at last upon a place
where I begin to face
our deaths. Begin
with the tallblack buildings
blocks that would mock
the laughter of a child.

                              Skyline Plaza

and routes with numbers
Pythagoras never dreamed
unless he knew everything.
Guzzles of gasoline nozzles
queer conversations
I can have out here
on this highway apart from myself
and far from you.

A softly lighted nightmare
along Glebe Road
where extra crispy is fifty cents
extra for light meat
and yellow fries are flung
for what could be
a mock celebration of the death
of the King of England.

An America that will never
be familiar
to you or me.
Was there ever an ocean or ever
a *before* here?
Hushed hands blessing the deer?

The trees it seems
dare not blossom thickly
for fear of censure
and property tax
increase. Minimalist
art but still a miracle
this April   month of beginnings.

Last Summer, Rehoboth Beach

We pray on gray days in the city
something has to sustain us
the dolphin's arc   black
with mystery   lithe   leaping and at last
gone. Sunset and a shy kiss.
                                             Death
is more bliss than we can remember.
We practice in the night   naked
with stars. Your dark
beginnings curve like mussels shells
open tossed by love   laid
in the sand. Oh I learn
your tongue   your hand.
Our flesh is fraught with the sea's foam

                                             and then

our own unbidden helpless spasm.

at home, inland

i'll settle for the oceans here
in the silver of tall maple branches
rushing beyond the borders of streets
swinging backward and forward
in the frenzies of wind
the sky is almost flat
not a myriad metamorphosing
protean   like harlequin
not bleeding like god.

but i am here
looking out through my window
and words are a spray of waves.
i will read to you
the wind   the leaves
the story of the boy in prison
whose still dark cell
seems convicted with frost
and hours overburdened with hope.
i will write
there are planets in orbit
too swift to feel.

flight to johannesburg

i was so much one
with the rage of time
i could not write
the story
of the blades impatiently slicing
the air   whirring
like my ambition
ahead of the wings

i could not see
the locket below my mother's
face where she keeps
my body's image
flinching with pain
and keeps her heart still
refusing to fail

                    obsessed with
                    the distant dreamer's vision
                    of starving millions of children
                    in soweto
                    i was fleeing the streets
                    of roxbury and columbus

i could not hear
the crack in my father's throat
the story of his own
fatherless life
his hunger
for what could never be

and i am left wondering now
whether when you're a poet
there's nothing private anymore
and everything matters
the propeller's purr
your lover's own
cries in the night

but the thing is
you can never read
a blade of grass   a butterfly's
twitter on the honied air
the beat of a heart
next to death
or the star's fall to life

you can never write
a poem without love

god's intricacies

my world is largely
without
creatures
and leaves
i have not seen
the moment where autumn ends
the year is accomplished and
winter begins
but in the cool blue
late august dawn
tokens
(and prophecies)
rise

the dead cicada's wings
poised   final
stride
no more
for love   they call
in another tongue
between
the curved lines of silence
these winding
country paths where you and i
have died
graced by green   your fingers
gently sworn

climb my aching
thighs   i cry
                    roads every-
          where
                    and curved
                              lines of wings.

Two For Lorraine
begun 1990

    1

The anguish of a visitor
is never the anguish
of the one who lives
there. The terror
of pre-dawn raids.
The empty table.
The thin heat
in the crowded room.

The one who remains
there turning
on a doubtful thread
of breath and air.

2

Sometimes the mind's rooms
are windowless. But time
is a thing of Earth. Termites
under the stony floor.

Soils erode and leaves
turn brown in revelation.
Cicadas sing all night
in misty fields.

Inkathazo*—or that Southern Cross above
makes human suffering seem grand.
Or our bodies could become the mirror
of Earth and Sky.

* *Inkathazo* is a Zulu word suggesting the cross that one
bears.

Translations From Vaclav Havel, 1992

We can no longer be
hollow-men
perpetually
between words
of epilogue and prologue
outliving principled princesses
of bartered kingdoms
cannot be
perpetually
ready
or even sublimely
lonely
like a god.
There is the alchemical hour
the sweep of syllables
on the sheet
and in the sky
and firmament-perplexed fingers
fighting
with the leanness of knives
drawing blood
drawing furrows in a field.
We weave
the canvas of a scene
where a pruning hook is
transformed
from a spear.
Yes a spear
is the inchoate curve
of the dream.

III
DIASPORA

diaspora

the first crazy person
i ever heard of that mattered
was my great aunt
cally
in tennessee. she never talked
much and looked
half-white but maybe
we all were crazy that way
with no more evening fires
flaming from the ground
like roots of trees
no more storytellers
hushing us with our
stories
no memory of jackals howling
except maybe for garbage.

aunt cally
shot uncle tom's dogs.
tom was her son
and almost young as me.
he cried
he shoulda shot them dogs
hisself he said
his wife skinny margaret
with a head full of hair
sent aunt cally to the state house
that's why i remember
since no one on the colored
side of town
ever went there

before
people just said
"niggers is crazy"
in those days
we still did just about everything
different
at wakes
everybody came
and snuck a little
hot sauce on their greens
and even at funerals
had no manners
carried on about what was lost
before it died.

Pride Parades

Washington, D.C.

As for most things that matter, like undying
flagrant falsehoods and other generosities,
these June queens have a penchant for names:
Mary Magdeline Gracelove, Gorgeous Gretchen and
Twiggy, but this one had boobs—and Baby,
I never saw such a thing in Johannesburg!
Ooh! I came over here to "come
out!" My sister said Soweto had enough problems
without me passing shebeens in clothes
that were brighter and sadder than hers.
And it's too hot there for my rouge to last!
Besides, it looks too much like the blood
that ran down my father's face
and into my hand. He wouldn't have liked
that—his bloody head in my painted hand.
It's not a country of Jordan Rivers,
just walls and watchdogs everywhere. They say
everything has its place. Our names til yesterday
were black, coloured, Indian and white
in colourless coffins beneath the passport stamp.

Now Is The Time Of Nostalgia

Take big Bessie Smith, loving
to sing the country of her varicose veins
or Georgia O'Keeffe's bones
on the chalky desert wall. The burst
of a dark orchid: Piaf!
Piaf! they would cry
and *The Blue Angel* still plays.

Abbey Lincoln moans. Somewhere
the *chansons* of Brel are belted,
lilted, and luring in rows
of smoky rooms where people lived
with terror, the edge
the other side
of beauty.

And a blackberry
wide-eyed woman child dreams
after school
in the local public library.
She meets a faded photograph
—some Josephine Baker, a gramophone
exotic tongue. She sees

the bronze flesh dancing, a stranger,
some kind of
mother.
She walks now unseen,
homeward, to her brothers
and supper of yellow corn,
sugared beans.

on "the mis-education of the negro"

dear carter woodson
i've been looking
at this film—*Sir Gawain
and the Green Knight.*
i never learned to pronounce
the knight's name.
i knew it sounded
foreign but to what?
i noticed that the villains were many
and dark and the hero wore gold
and white. some say,
ah that is merely
physical. you must look
deeper for the spiritual meaning.
and do not look into history
god's covenant
with the afrikaner and the curses
visited on abyssinia.
do not look
to the kkk
or death row or the red
flood of the mississippi.
i sense this is not
necessarily
a film for popcorn and butter
but there is love
to be sure in the unattainable
virgin. then

the commercial selling perfume
always appears in-between

just when the swords are raised
to another octave and heaven
is about to be revealed
or maybe the lenses are threatening
hell. so i had no time
to wonder if i could ride
through those northern forests
or hold my breath til the magic
might find me—pure
as a pale flower.
no mind to guess whether
my tangled black hair
and hungry lips   my heritage
of a vagrant great grandmother
—burning with his bible
and his whip—excluded me.

story

there is this story
of the african
woman
you understand
who just became bored
with her own near
perfection
she had learned to stand
just about anything
                    alligators' snaps from sleep
                    pots of river water
                    weighing on her head
                    drums signalling the gods'
                    displeasure   babies
                    buried from smallpox
                    a clip in the place of too much
                    pleasure
                    war as the price of chastity
                    public rite as the price
                    of woman love
                    or the other wives'
                    suspicious eyes
                    measuring the grain in her pots
she could stand
it all
and so
when the hirsute strangers came
and one slammed her scars
with the silvered butt of his gun
and took her child
to the edge of forever

she did not know the name
of her newest anguish
the flung ellipse of her mind
she did not know
she was supposed
to fall down and die.

HOW CAN YOU COGITATE WITH BLEACHED
MILLIPAP AND INFESTED WATER?*

I plead for programs and ration-
al critiques by my own people.
But the latest book on Azania
is sickled over
with pale northern reason
so unlike the restless sun
on the sorghum
field or the chameleon plodding
on the country road   or the moon
hanging in your womb.
So unlike the teeth of township
youth biting at themselves
and the yellow air. So unlike
the night's mosquito madness
or a man faltering
from mother to daughter
in the cramped ocean
of a one-room shack.
                              I forget
what Fanon   Robeson
Maxine Waters   Ayi
Kwei Armah   and Bessie Head
never forget
entering Los Angeles or Serowe
or Antigua like it's home.
I think they understand
how we traveled

* Millipap is a form of finely ground corn and is today a
commercially adapted cheap staple food eaten by South
Africans.

so far away from ourselves
and ended up
laughing at the praying mantis.
How we heard the admiral's finger
as the starched white snap.

But the seers remember the shapes
of land and wind and the people's
need for rage, the body's history
and hunger for more than bread.

a letter i cannot post to atteridgeville*

i read your smuggled letter
i take the gift you give
like your sotho name
and the news they print
is just plain wrong
about change
i don't trust poetry
tonight   what metaphor
will survive beside
your words?

they follow me you say
who?
follow our family   why?
how can you know?
what do they
think you know?
those ghosts
in the tower in ties?

you've pulled back
from the organization
themba too
he cannot
concentrate on law
school   too many phantoms
like flying ants around his head
so he took the money

* atteridgeville is a site of enforced segregation, a black
township in the region of pretoria, south africa

and bought a taxi
to transport the workers
and who knows who
the kilometres to pretoria

how many stones
does white millipap and murder
make?
how many children
have you miscarried
in the flood
of township blood?

you write
we are living through
the worst time of our lives
your neighbor gunned down
fifteen minutes after
he left your living room
not trust hangs
on the edges of language
like a beggar

your children that remain
must find
a way to school
maybe they will sing
a different song of power
light a candle
they brought from another world

Can I Speak With You, Irina Ratushinskaya?

My poems are troubled translations
from the Russian in a Kiev jail
or Quiché curses in Spanish, or Sesotho
screams. From the odor
of blood, and over here
the candles in the sacristy
of a place fated
for an ancient saint.

I can no longer speak
luxuries, no longer
meet my mother's lips, nor slowly
write. The bell
might ring anytime, the gun pop
as though life
were a thing like the jerk
of a ragged clock.
                                Let us stop now
and listen. The rain is tender and cold
on the last of the leaves.
For your fingers
a cup of cider.
I want to say
remember
all the colors
of burning and blood
—and (quite enough,
in spite of all)
whatever the sun
hiding
will yield.

Looking For What Is Native

open this sound
—Meridel Le Sueur

I become sick if I go too long without
listening to a poem. I read but must hear it
in my mind like a sacramental hum
or the morning buzz of bees in the grass
before the lawnmower kills. I remember

another traffic. The sound of Harjo talking
of little moments near Albuquerque
when the Earth was still
hot with horses. And I said
"good-bye, I love you," and you answered

"good-bye," smiling. I did not notice
my uncertainties hanging on your smile,
the splinters of fear in my left breast,
the flicker of a wish to be, let go
my official-self with lock and key.

All this is what comes.
Listen. A poem is
the sun's sizzle singing
to our fears. This when the Earth
was hot with horses.